Original title:
Tying the Heartstrings

Copyright © 2025 Creative Arts Management OÜ
All rights reserved.

Author: Dante Kingsley
ISBN HARDBACK: 978-1-80586-216-1
ISBN PAPERBACK: 978-1-80586-688-6

Embracing Fragility

Delicate bonds that squeeze so tight,
We laugh as we bumble through the night.
A heart so soft, it's hard to keep,
Like juggling cats while trying to sleep.

Emotions bounce like rubber balls,
A cosmic joke within four walls.
We trip on love, the clumsy dance,
And lose ourselves in a silly glance.

Knotted Fates

Two strings twist in a comic show,
Tripping on fate, where will we go?
Like socks in a dryer, they spin around,
Tangled in laughter, joy profound.

Life's a knot that often slips,
We make a toast with clumsy sips.
The more we tug, the tighter it gets,
But with every pull, more laughter begets.

The Language of Yearning

We whisper wishes on the breeze,
Sounding like a swarm of bees.
Each yearn and sigh a goofy sound,
Our hearts speak fluent fool-around.

With every giggle, love unfolds,
In clumsy texts and stories told.
The goofy charms that we employ,
Are codes of our quirky joy.

Shadows of Affection

In shadows where the chuckles grow,
Our hearts reflect a funny glow.
A slapstick hug, a silly wink,
In whispers that make the heart rethink.

We dance like penguins, slip and slide,
Through hallways where our laughter hides.
Each shadow holds a playful spark,
In love's sweet folly, we find our mark.

The Knot of Reminiscence

Once I tripped, fell for you,
Tangled laughs, oh what a view,
We laughed so hard, it was a scene,
Who knew love could be so keen?

Misplaced socks and silly chats,
Whiskers on our playful cats,
Nostalgic tales with goofy flair,
Memories woven, none compare.

Chords of the Heart

Strumming funny tunes so bright,
Dancing wildly through the night,
Your clumsy moves, oh what a sight,
Love's odd rhythms bring delight.

Crispy snacks and drink spills too,
You giggled hard while I just blew,
We played our hearts like silly strings,
Life's sweet lullaby, laughter sings.

The Loom of Affection

Weaving tales with quirk and glee,
Each thread holds a mystery,
Silly hats and mismatched shoes,
Our quirky vibes, we always choose.

Oh, how you dance like no one sees,
Twisting fate on a gentle breeze,
With every laugh, we spin our tales,
In our little world, joy prevails.

Heartfelt Connections

Through jumbled words and silly jokes,
Our bond's alive, it truly pokes,
With every giggle, love's reflected,
In clumsy chaos, we're connected.

You stole my fries, I stole your heart,
Funny moments are our art,
With shared smiles, our jokes take flight,
Together we shine, oh what a sight!

Heartfelt Knots

Roses are red, violets are blue,
I tripped on my love, now I'm stuck like glue.
Wrapped up in laughter, like a burrito tight,
We giggle and wiggle into the night.

You stole my fries, a heart in disguise,
With ketchup-smeared kisses, it's love on the rise.
In this silly tango of laughter and glee,
Who knew romance could come with a spree?

The Dance of Intimacy

Two left feet, but we dance like pros,
When you spin me 'round, I can't feel my toes.
We step on each other and laugh till we cry,
In this clumsy ballet, we take to the sky.

Your partner's so charming, a sight quite surreal,
With a twist and a turn, our joy is our meal.
A pirouette here, and a dip over there,
Who knew waltzing could lead to a snare?

Stitches of Memory

We stitched up our past with mismatched thread,
Each memory woven, enough to be fed.
From quirky adventures on bicycles too,
To the time you fell and tried to woo me anew.

Laughter like patches on our quilt of delight,
Sewn tight with mischief, we conquer the night.
A stitch in the heart, it keeps us both warm,
Our whims keep us close, through every storm.

Moored by Love

In a boat of our dreams, we float and we sway,
With banana peels and giggles, we paddle away.
Anchored in humor, our ship sails so free,
Together we navigate this crazy sea.

You're the wind in my sails, blowing sweet and loud,
With waves of laughter, we dance like a crowd.
Caught in your laughter, I drift and I dream,
Our hearts are the compass, together we beam.

Knotted Dreams

In a land where socks play hide and seek,
A cat steals my lunch with a sly little peek.
We dance through the chaos, wearing mismatched shoes,
Laughing at life and the silly things we choose.

The spaghetti's tangled, like thoughts in my head,
I trip on my shoelaces, a comedy thread.
With a wink and a grin, we wobble around,
Making memories, as we tumble down.

The Fabric of Us

In quilted moments, patches of glee,
We stitch together laughter, just you and me.
A button pops off while we share a drink,
As we giggle at threads that no one would think.

Our brushes are clumsy, colors collide,
Sprinkles of joy; we wear with pride.
The fabric of life, an ever-spun tale,
With stitches of humor that never will fail.

Interlaced Whispers

In a world of jumbled words and strange tweets,
We whisper our secrets, while munching on sweets.
Your puns are like magic, they twist and they twirl,
Creating a symphony with each little swirl.

Our thoughts interwoven, like hair in a braid,
Each laugh a small spark that will never degrade.
Together we're chaos, a musical score,
As we dance through the night, always wanting more.

Bonds Unseen

In shadows we chuckle, like pals at a show,
With blunders and mishaps that no one may know.
We juggle our dreams with a comical twist,
Crafting a chaos that can't be dismissed.

With rubber bands stretched and paper clips bent,
Our lives make a melody, a sweet accident.
In this playful mess, we'll forever entwine,
As partners in giggles, both silly and fine.

Weaving Love's Tapestry

I stitched a heart with thread so bright,
But it unraveled in the night.
My sewing skills, quite a mess,
Should have opted for a dress!

Each knot I tied brought laughter loud,
But I tripped on my own proud.
Now love's a patchwork, full of cheer,
With a funny quilt that we both wear.

Bonds that Bind

We started off with shoelace ties,
But now we've got spaghetti flies.
A tangled mess of pasta dreams,
Wrapped up tightly at the seams.

We giggled as we fell in sync,
In this embrace, we laugh and wink.
Somehow the sauce is what we need,
For a flavorful bond, indeed!

Chords of the Soul

Plucked a string—what a weird sound,
Like a cat in a sock, all around.
Yet through the chaos, music plays,
In our hearts, it stays and sways.

We dance to tones that make no sense,
A symphony of our difference.
Each note a chuckle, each beat a grin,
With laughter, we simply begin.

Sorrow's Embrace

She wore a frown shaped like a pie,
While I attempted to bake her a lie.
Flour in the air, tears in the bowl,
Who knew a cake could take such a toll?

With a chocolate swirl, things got bright,
Sorrow's embrace gave way to delight.
Together we laughed, a sweet little spree,
Over frosting and crumbs, just her and me.

Love's Latticework

In the garden of quirks we dance,
With peanut butter and a fleeting glance.
You trip, I laugh, the joke's on me,
Our love's a mess, yet we feel so free.

With puzzle pieces that don't quite fit,
We build strange castles, a perfect split.
You snore like a bear, it makes me giggle,
Our hearts entwined, they wiggle and wriggle.

Affection's Embrace

Your socks mismatch, but who really cares?
Fashion faux pas, yet love always shares.
We dance in the kitchen, burnt toast in hand,
With flour on noses, our life feels so grand.

The cat thinks we're nuts, and I guess she's right,
We argue like kids, but it feels so bright.
Your quirky style makes the world seem new,
Two jesters in love, a marvelous view.

The Symphony of Us

Two silly notes in a jazzy tune,
I cook you dinner; it's burned—oh, soon!
Yet laughter rings out, like a sweet refrain,
Together we dance through sunshine and rain.

You pick my brain while I steal your fries,
With googly eyes, we both make a prize.
Life's a ballet, with all its full flaws,
Our comedy plays, with half-hearted applause.

Heartstrings in Harmony

In the symphony of laughter, we find our way,
With silly faces that brighten the day.
You bring the punchline, I hold the cue,
In the grandest show, we're the funniest two.

With mismatched socks and a wobbly chair,
We create a world without any care.
Through gaffes and giggles, our love shines bright,
A circus of hearts, we soar with delight.

The Dance of Connection

In the ballroom of life, we trip and sway,
Stumbling on words we wish to say.
With two left feet, we kick up dust,
Dancing in circles, it's all a must.

Laughter erupts with each little spin,
When we spin away, then right back in.
But in this waltz of the hearts entwined,
It's the missteps that leave joy behind.

Threads of Affection

Pulling at strings that sometimes snap,
Creating a quilt, oh what a trap!
With flimsy fabric, we sew our fate,
Laughing at how we can coordinate.

Each stitch a joke, in the fabric of time,
It's a patchwork of memories, oh so sublime.
But if the needle pricks a little too deep,
We'll laugh it off, no time for sleep.

Weaving Emotions

Looms are clattering, colors in flight,
We weave our tales deep into the night.
With threads of joy and spools of delight,
Our tapestry sparkles, a shared insight.

Mistakes are colors, they brighten the thread,
A splash here and there, enough to spread.
In this crafty mess, laughter takes helm,
Creating a quilt, it's our little realm.

When Souls Embrace

A hug's a squish, not always sheer bliss,
Sometimes we stumble, can't help but miss.
Yet in that chaos, a chuckle's in store,
Wrapped up in warmth, still begging for more.

Each squeeze tells tales of moments so true,
Like a friendly bear, I'd cuddle you too.
In this silly dance, our humor's the key,
Embracing the awkward, just you and me.

Soulful Strings

In a noodle shop, I found my muse,
Slurping sounds, no time to snooze.
Your laughter caught, a playful tease,
I offered you my last piece of cheese.

You said, 'This isn't love, just food!'
But every bite just set the mood.
With quirky jokes, the night would weave,
A tapestry of fun, you'd never believe.

In the Warmth of Connection

Two chairs in the park, we won't sit still,
Your humor's bright, it gives me a thrill.
I bumped your soda, oh what a mess,
You laughed so hard, it caused distress.

We shared a pie, a cherry delight,
With whipped cream splashes, oh what a sight!
You said, 'It's a date!' with a wink and a grin,
Our hearts do the tango, let the fun begin!

The Echo of Us

In a karaoke bar, you stole the show,
Off-key notes, but with gusto to glow.
You whispered, 'Is this romance or a joke?'
Then danced like a chicken, and I nearly choked.

We sang our hearts out, two clumsy ducks,
With laughter that sparked, who needs good luck?
Your silly moves echoed in my heart,
A lighthearted dance, a perfect start!

Weaving Dreams Together

At the craft store, we found our fate,
Yarn tangled up, it's quite the trait.
You said, 'Let's knit a scarf for my cat!'
But the stitches flew wild, oh imagine that!

We crafted chaos, a colorful spree,
With glitter and laughter, just you and me.
As creation fell apart, we both did agree,
Our messy art was the best kind of glee!

Intertwined Destinies

Two socks that lost their way,
Find each other in the fray.
One is red, the other blue,
Together they make quite a crew.

Wobbly chairs that dance and sway,
They tango during the day.
With every squeak, a laugh erupts,
In the chaos, love disrupts.

Mismatched spoons that laugh out loud,
In the drawer, they are quite proud.
They clink and clank like old-time friends,
Their playful game never ends.

A cat and dog, a silly pair,
Chasing tails without a care.
Together they make mischief thrive,
In this madness, we feel alive.

Secrets in Serenity

A turtle whispers to a snail,
"Let's race, but don't turn pale!"
A squirrel giggles from a tree,
"Who'll win? It's a mystery!"

Two teacups have a gossip fest,
Spilling secrets, they just jest.
One says, "Did you see her dance?"
The other laughs, "What a chance!"

A pillow fights with a soft shoe,
"No need to be so mad at you!"
They bounce and tumble with such glee,
In this quiet oddity.

The curtains sway with a cheeky breeze,
Tickling noses, bringing ease.
In this calm, a ruckus brews,
Oh, the laughter that ensues!

Delicate Bonds

A pair of glasses on the shelf,
Argue 'bout who sees themselves.
"Without me, you're just a blur!"
But still together, they prefer.

Morning coffee, a steamy duo,
Sipping tales of where they'll go.
One says, "Let's brew something new!"
The other laughs, "I'm up for two!"

Two balloons float beyond the gate,
One's a bit shy, the other's fate.
They bounce along with dreams in tow,
In the air, their colors glow.

Tangled headphones in a bag,
"Why are we always such a drag?"
Though a mess, they can't complain,
In the tangle, love's insane.

Echoes of Togetherness

A quirky snail and his best friend,
They race to see who'll reach the end.
One is slow, the other fast,
Laughing at how time is cast.

A feathered hat on a rabbit's head,
Makes him feel like he's misled.
He struts around the meadow wide,
With a flair he cannot hide.

Dancing spoons in a silver pot,
Laughing loudly, like it or not.
They jive away to a jazzy beat,
This cheerful chaos is quite the treat.

In this room, the magic flows,
Friendships bloom as laughter grows.
With every hiccup, every cheer,
Together we conquer every fear.

Knotting Memories

In the attic, dust does dance,
Old photos smile, given a chance.
Grandma's wig, a sight so grand,
Tangled laughter, hand in hand.

The kite we flew fell in a tree,
A squirrel laughed, so wild and free.
Chasing dreams, our socks mismatched,
Each little mishap perfectly patched.

A game of tag on muddy grounds,
With goofy grins, oh how it sounds!
Jumping puddles, splashing fun,
Memories made, never undone.

Whispers of Connection

Two cups clink in the morning light,
Your face smeared with peanut delight.
Whispers shared beneath the sun,
With giggles popping, joy's begun.

When pranks unfold in silly ways,
Like cream on noses, laughter stays.
Tickling tales of things we do,
In every mishap, bonds grew true.

The dance we did in mismatched shoes,
Twisted twirls, we couldn't lose!
Under the stars, we laughed and spun,
In whispered secrets, our hearts had fun.

Threads of Affection

A patchwork quilt of yesteryears,
Stitched with laughter, soaked in tears.
Crooked seams and colors bright,
Each square a memory, pure delight.

The cat's mischief, a tangled yarn,
Chasing tales from dusk till dawn.
A dance-off in our living room,
With every step, we shook the gloom.

Candy wrappers in a trail,
Adventures mapped with every fail.
Silly hats and goofy masks,
In these moments, joy just basks.

The Fabric of Emotions

Stitches made of easy laughs,
Funny faces, silly gaffes.
A pillow fight before bedtimes,
Feathered giggles, silly rhymes.

With jump ropes tied in a big knot,
Remembering every slip and plot.
Silly dances in the kitchen,
Step on toes? With joy, we're glitchin'.

A sock puppet with googly eyes,
Telling tales, oh what a surprise!
With each thread woven through our days,
Love's fabric wraps in the funniest ways.

Bouquet of Feelings

In a garden where giggles bloom,
Laughter dances, fills the room.
Petals tickle with funny sights,
Jokes and puns take off in flights.

A daisy winks at a busy bee,
While roses play in a silly spree.
Tulips wear hats all askew,
Blooms that chuckle, just for you.

Sunflowers stretch in the sunlight,
Cracking jokes from dawn till night.
The violets mumble secrets low,
A floral chorus in a show.

Gather these blooms, a joyful mess,
Each petal's charm, no need to stress.
With smiles and laughter intertwined,
A cheerful bouquet, love defined.

Sanctuary of Emotions

In a fort made of pillows high,
Where giggles soar and worries fly.
A blanket fort, our secret space,
Where silliness can win the race.

Cushions wave like flags of cheer,
As laughter echoes, crystal clear.
Whispers shared with a twist of glee,
Silly faces and a cup of tea.

Stuffed bears sit in solemn rows,
Giving hugs when the laughter flows.
Each chuckle cushions every fall,
In this cute haven, we have it all.

So let's laugh through every tear,
In our sanctuary, there's no fear.
Where hearts connect in the silliest way,
A fortress of joy where we can play.

Bridges of Understanding

Two squirrels chitchat on a line,
Sharing secrets and jokes so fine.
With acorns tossed, they find their way,
Building bridges of laughter each day.

Each giggle forms a pathway clear,
Mismatched socks bring goofy cheer.
Nutty plans bounce like springy strings,
Together they dance, oh what joy it brings!

To understand is to laugh aloud,
Finding common ground in a silly crowd.
With each pun that hops and skips,
They forge connections like playful flips.

So let's bridge the gaps with laughter bright,
Through funny tales and pure delight.
In this quirky world we've made, you see,
Understanding blooms, just let it be!

Threads of Fate

A spider spins in a silly way,
Crafting webs that dance and sway.
Tangled threads that twist and twirl,
Weaving laughs in a playful swirl.

Each line strums a comical song,
In the fabric of life, we all belong.
Snags and knots, a card trick fun,
Our fate's a game we all have won.

Laughter threads through every seam,
Silly accidents, a shared dream.
Fate lightly tugs at our sleeve,
In vibrant colors, we believe.

So let's dance upon this frayed line,
In a tapestry where we intertwine.
With humor brimming, bright and free,
Threads of fate weave our harmony.

The Weight of Whispered Promises

In a garden where secrets grow,
A rosebud blushes with a glow.
But promise me, please don't forget,
Last week's pizza, I'll never regret.

With whispers soft like cotton candy,
We share our dreams, a little dandy.
Yet every night, the truth unwinds,
Remembering socks, we cannot find.

Your laugh is like a small surprise,
It dances 'round like fireflies.
But in this circus, wild and free,
Your jokes are worse than my old knee.

When one slips up and makes a fuss,
I'll pull you back on the funny bus.
With winks and nods, we'll make it through,
Just keep the snacks, and I'll hug you too.

Emblems of Intimacy

Two cups of coffee, side by side,
A toast to quirks, to love and pride.
We giggle at an inside joke,
Like cats who plot, and then provoke.

You steal my fries, oh what a heist,
Yet I can't be too mad, not quite, not sliced.
Your goofy grin warms my heart,
In this dance, we both play our part.

In matching socks, we strut and sway,
As silly hats do lead the way.
An emblem shared, this bond we wear,
A badge of laughter, light as air.

Through all the chaos, loud and bright,
Our laughter glows against the night.
So grab a snack, stay by my side,
In this funny ride, we'll take the tide.

Sculpture of Sentiments

With clay of dreams, we mold our fate,
A heart-shaped bowl, it's not too late.
Giggles echo through the air,
As we create with just a flair.

Your goofy pose, a master's touch,
In every squish, I love you so much.
We sculpt together, laugh and fumble,
In this artistry, we shall not tumble.

Our masterwork, a lopsided face,
Yet in its flaws, we find our place.
With silly grins, we trade and share,
Each little quirk—a masterpiece rare.

So raise your hands, let's give a cheer,
For humor's dance that draws us near.
In every layer, laughter blends,
A sculpture where the love transcends.

Bonds Beyond Time

In a world where clocks behave,
We lost the time that we once gave.
Yet every giggle, every jest,
Rewinds the clock—we feel so blessed.

When life gets tough, we trade the woes,
With silly hats and nosy crows.
Our hearts entwined in a jigsaw game,
Each piece a chuckle, never the same.

So hop along this funky train,
Counting moments, not the strain.
In the buffet of love, we dine,
With each silly dish, your heart in mine.

The years may fly like birds on wing,
But in our laughter, we'll always sing.
For bonds like ours, so sweet and fine,
Are timeless treasures, a grand design.

Unraveled Hearts

In the circus of romance, we all take a spin,
With clumsy tightrope acts, we trip and we grin.
Three clowns on a date, juggling hearts in the air,
One drops a balloon, and we all stop and stare.

With love as our guide, we dance in the rain,
Splashing in puddles, forgetting the pain.
A heart-shaped balloon floats away with a squeak,
We laugh at our folly, 'till next week, next week!'

Subtle Connections

Two hearts in a café, sipping tea with a twist,
Mistaking their orders, a caffeinated tryst.
She gets his espresso, he bites on her cake,
They giggle at blunders, they muffle a quake.

Through winks and odd glances, a spark starts to glow,
Like fireflies twirling, in an unplanned show.
Wrong numbers and jokes, oh the laughter resounds,
In this tangled connection, joy knows no bounds.

The Ties that Enfold

In a world made of noodles, our hearts intertwine,
Like spaghetti and meatballs, it's all so divine.
We twirl and we tangle, we splatter with sauce,
A plateful of giggles, no reason to pause.

Two friends in mismatched socks, a comedy scene,
Tripping over their feet, like a dance that's unseen.
Yet out of the chaos, sweet harmony flows,
In each silly moment, true friendship just grows.

Navigating Emotions

We sail on a boat, made of paper and dreams,
Through rivers of laughter, we paddle in teams.
A map filled with tickles, leads us where we play,
With sinking and drifting, we're lost on our way.

At the helm of our ship, a captain so bold,
With socks on his hands, and a heart made of gold.
Through storms of absurdity, we keep riding high,
In this ocean of whimsy, we'll never say die.

A Symphony of Strings

When life gives you silly strings,
Just pull and see what chaos brings.
A banjo here, a fiddle there,
We dance and laugh, without a care.

The cat joins in, he steals the show,
With a meow that steals the flow.
He thinks he's part of our grand band,
As I try to keep my coffee stand.

Harmonicas buzz as we skip and hop,
It's all a game that never stops.
With laughter bright, we hold our tune,
On this crazy afternoon!

So let the notes fly high and free,
In this wacky act of unity.
With strings that twist and turn around,
A symphony of joy is found.

The Melody of Togetherness

We made a band with pots and spoons,
Our jam sessions start at noon.
Dancing socks and clanging bowls,
Creating music that shakes our soles.

Your goofy smile makes the notes shine,
As off-key echoes intertwine.
We sing about the bread we burn,
And all those lessons that we learn.

A musical dish, a rhythm of laughs,
With silly faces and crooked drafts.
Our hearts would play the sweetest tune,
As popcorn pops and dances to the moon.

So grab a spoon, and join the fun,
In this melody, we're all as one.
With every beat, our spirits soar,
Together we'll create and explore!

Hearts in Harmony

In a room where echoes spree,
We create melodies joyfully.
You play the kazoo, I hum along,
Strumming laughter all night long.

Silly hats and mismatched shoes,
We prance around, sharing our blues.
Every snort and giggle ignites,
Our hearts align like endless flights.

With a rubber chicken as our muse,
We harmonize with improvises.
Your quirkiness, my absent mind,
In this musical, we're intertwined.

So let's raise a toast to this funny crew,
With every note, laughter feels brand new.
We're a circus show, no need for cues,
Hearts in sync, letting joy ensue!

Tapestry of Longing

With threads of laughter, we create,
A tapestry of fun, never late.
Each stitch a story, brightly spun,
In this fabric of friends, we've won.

Your quirks are treasures, stitch by stitch,
As we weave together without a hitch.
With every loop, our tale unwinds,
As we share secrets and silly signs.

A canvas bright, with colors bold,
Strung with dreams that never grow old.
We mend our hearts with goofy grace,
Through tangled threads, we find our place.

So here's to giggles, to heartfelt seams,
In this tapestry, we chase our dreams.
With laughter spun into the night,
Together we twinkle, a cozy sight.

Echoes of Intimacy

In the park where lovers meet,
A squirrel sneaks snacks, oh what a treat!
They steal glances, shy and sweet,
But trip on laces, fall at their feet.

Giggles burst from a hidden tree,
As butterflies dance, wild and free.
He drops his ice cream, oh what a sight,
She laughs so hard, it feels just right.

They play tag in a game of fate,
But his shoelace knotted, it won't be straight.
He yanks and pulls, what a crazy whirl,
She can't stop giggling, what a perfect twirl!

Love's echoes dance in the air tonight,
As joyful memories take off in flight.
With a wink and a smile, they find their way,
In this silly game, they choose to stay.

Fabricating Love

In a workshop of hearts, they play with glue,
Creating affection, what a thing to do!
Laughter erupts over tangled yarns,
As they try to craft their romantic charms.

He accidentally sticks her to the floor,
"Oops!" she giggles, "But wait, there's more!"
With a painted smile and a lopsided grin,
They fashion love where the laughter begins.

A spool of humor, thread of delight,
Their hands create magic, all through the night.
With each silly slip and playful glance,
They weave a tapestry of a goofy romance.

In every mishap, a bond starts to grow,
Fabricating moments, love's subtle flow.
With glue and giggles, their hearts interlace,
Building a world filled with joy and grace.

Unraveled Secrets

Peeking through curtains, the secrets unveil,
Puppies and kittens join in the tale.
Whispers of joy, oh what a delight,
With noodle limbs tangled in soft moonlight.

Under the covers, a tickle-fight spree,
Giggling and hiding, where could they be?
Twirls of confusion, socks mismatched,
In the chaos of laughter, their hearts are attached.

With a dash of whimsy and a splash of fun,
They share ice cream, but oh, it's a run!
The sprinkles rain down like silly confetti,
Each scoop a sweet secret, sugar ready.

Those puzzling moments, they make the best lore,
Where love's little quirks come knocking at the door.
Through giggles and whispers, they start to unlace,
In the tapestry woven, they find their embrace.

The Stitch of Sentiment

With needle in hand, they sew up a tale,
A patchwork of moments that never grow stale.
Each stitch a giggle, a wink, or a nudge,
In the quilt of their hearts, they happily trudge.

Silly mischief turns into a thread,
With laughter embroidered all through their bed.
He spills the beans, she stitches it tight,
Creating a bond in the soft, starry night.

Through the fabric of time, they patch up their dreams,
In a world stitched together with laughter, it seems.
Sparks of affection, oh what a riot,
Every little quirk, a love-fueled diet.

So here's to the stitches that bind, so divine,
In the crazy quilt of hearts, they intertwine.
With playful banter and love that won't budge,
They find joy reflected in each silly smudge.

Churning Currents of Emotion

In a boat made of giggles, we drift with glee,
Paddling through puddles, just you and me.
With waves of laughter crashing so bright,
Who knew emotions could feel so light?

A splash of confusion, a drizzle of fun,
We're tangled in chaos, oh what have we done?
But in every whirlpool, I find you there,
Like socks in the dryer, a curious pair.

As currents collide, we dance on the foam,
Navigating this sea, oh how far we've grown.
With a wink and a grin, we steer our own fate,
In churning emotions, we float, never wait.

So here's to our voyage, aboard this odd ship,
With laughter as our compass, and a snack for the trip.
We'll surf on the waves, wave at the shore,
In the churning of life, I couldn't ask for more.

The Serenade of Love

Under a sky made of cotton candy haze,
We hum silly tunes that leave us in a daze.
With a kazoo chorus, and shimmies to spare,
Our serenade echoes, turning heads everywhere.

You dance on my toes, like it's part of the plan,
But what's with that move? It looks like a sham!
Yet here comes the laughter, it fills all the air,
Our quirky duet, more fun than a bear.

In a world full of roses, we're daisies instead,
With petals of humor, where mischief is bred.
No candlelit dinner, just popcorn and puns,
In this sweet serenade, we jest and we run.

So let's strum our hearts, with a banjo of grin,
The melody's goofy, but oh let's dive in!
For in this wild opera, our laughter's the cue,
In the serenade of love, it's just me and you.

Interwoven Lives

Like spaghetti and meatballs, we twist and we twirl,
In a pot of absurdity, we give it a whirl.
Each strand that connects us, a flavor so bold,
Together we simmer, our friendship a gold.

With socks that are mismatched, we strut down the street,
You wear my old hat, what a laugh, what a feat!
In this quilt of our lives, we patch up each tear,
With stitches of banter, a pattern so rare.

A sprinkle of hiccups, a drizzle of grace,
In the jigsaw of chaos, we find our own place.
From morning coffee spills to late-night snacks,
Our interwoven journey, with plenty of laughs.

So here's to our threads, tangled yet neat,
With a tapestry woven, our lives are a treat.
In the loom of existence, we weave and we dive,
Embracing the chaos, we sparkle alive!

Ethereal Connections

In a land made of giggles and dragonfly wings,
We bounce on the clouds, like the silliest things.
With whispers of whimsy, we dance through the air,
Our ethereal bond is beyond compare.

You twirled like a leaf in a whirlpool of fun,
A laugh like a firework, bursting and done.
As stars burst in laughter, we chuckle so bright,
What magic brings two goofballs to light?

With glimmers of mischief, we soar through the night,
Chasing our shadows until morning light.
In this cosmic ballet, where wackiness reclaims,
Our connection's a canvas, where humor frames.

So let's leap through the galaxies, shout out our cheer,
With a wink and a giggle, in this atmosphere.
For in the vast universe, where silliness sways,
Ethereal connections hold laughter always!

The Web of Souls

In a café of fate, we sip our brew,
A bond made from laughter, just me and you.
With tales of our mishaps, the spills and thrills,
We're tangled in giggles, against life's drills.

Like spaghetti on plates, we twist and twine,
Sharing all secrets over glasses of wine.
With quirks that unravel, we dance and we play,
In this web of connection, we find our way.

Your jokes are like fireworks, bright in the night,
We're chums in this circus, both silly and bright.
With a wink and a nudge, you know just what to say,
In this jumbled comedy, we'll never stray.

So raise up your cup, let's toast to the fun,
To the ties that we cherish, that bright morning sun.
In this web we have woven, let laughter entwine,
Forever in jest, your heart will be mine.

Twilight Threads

In the twilight of nonsense, we start to create,
Threads of our stories, oh isn't it great?
Like a jumbled-up puzzle, a hairball of luck,
We stumble and chuckle, what's your next quirk?

With puns flying freely, like stars in the sky,
We tease and we giggle, just you and I.
Each moment a stitch in our fabric of fun,
We craft our own mischief till day's finally done.

Your tales are delightfully absurd, oh my!
Like shoes on a cat that's prepared for a fly.
As twilight descends, we waltz in our haze,
Chasing dreams in this madness, we're lost in a craze.

So wear that strange hat, let's prance through the dark,
With laughter a beacon, igniting our spark.
In this fabric of twilight, where whimsy sings loud,
We're bound by our humor, forever proud.

Whispers Across Time

In the whispers of ages, we stumble and glide,
Through centuries giggling, on this wild ride.
With legends that tickle, from past to our now,
We're messengers of fun, take a bow, take a bow.

Oh, the time travelers' blunders, a sight to behold,
In togas and rags, our laughter is bold.
From cavemen to wizards, we banter and jest,
With a wink and a grin, we're having the best.

With relics of humor, we giggle and cheer,
To connect through the ages, my friend, hold me near.
Each whisper a bond that we never outgrow,
Our hearts intertwined like the roots of a tree, whooa!

So here's to the laughter that stands the test of time,
To the echoes of joy that rhythm and rhyme.
In this dance of the centuries, let's celebrate,
With whispers of laughter, it's never too late.

Unraveled Euphoria

In the chaos of joy, we frolic and roll,
Each heartbeat a giggle, a shared little goal.
With sips of sweet silliness, we spill on the floor,
Unraveled euphoria, oh, give me some more!

With quirky connections that bounce off the wall,
We pirouette through life and have a ball.
As marshmallows fly, and the confetti drops,
Our hearts are the piñatas, bursting in hops.

You dance like a penguin, I jump like a frog,
In this circus of bliss, we're lost in the fog.
With humor that sparkles and shines like the sun,
Unraveled, unhinged, our fun's just begun.

So here's to these moments, absurd as they seem,
Let's ride this wild wave, in our wonderful dream.
In this jumbled-up journey, my dear, hold me tight,
Euphoria's our compass, let's soar in delight!

Essence of Togetherness

In a café, we share a slice,
Your crumbs fall down, oh, what a price!
Laughter spills like soda pop,
Together, we'll never stop.

With socks that don't quite match at all,
We strut down streets, have a ball.
Dancing like no one can see,
Clumsy moves, just you and me.

Collecting quirks, we start a show,
Our secret handshake, quite the flow.
Each little quibble, a story told,
Our bond is silly and bold.

In this circus, we play our part,
With joy that dances in the heart.
So grab my hand, let's take a chance,
In this goofy, wild romance!

Weaving Light and Shadows

Two shadows chatting on a wall,
One's super tall, the other small.
A game of tag among the beams,
Fitting laughter into dreams.

We hide behind the movie screens,
Crafting stories, laughing scenes.
Popcorn flying in dismay,
Together, we'll save the day.

Then off we trot to find some food,
A daring quest to change our mood.
Spaghetti twirling on a fork,
Who knew that food could make us snort?

Dancing 'round on lazy days,
Making fun in so many ways.
In every mishap, there's a cheer,
Together, my friend, let's find our gear!

Tapestry of Longing

A sock that's missing brings a sigh,
In laundry chaos, let's not cry.
We'll knit our laughs like yarn so bright,
Creating warmth through silly fights.

The pizza's burnt, the drinks are spilled,
Yet here we sit, and I'm thrilled.
Giggling 'bout our kitchen fails,
Our friendship's worth is in the tales.

Jumping puddles on the street,
Splashing laughter, what a treat!
Sometimes we fumble, sometimes we rhyme,
But every moment feels like prime.

With goofy hats and silly faces,
We navigate through life's embraces.
In this tapestry of our fun,
Our threads are tangled, but we're one!

The Unseen Embrace

Invisible hugs in crowded rooms,
Nonsense chatter, quirky fumes.
With a wink, we share a thought,
In the laughter, joy is sought.

Magic beans in coffee cups,
The giggles rise, then bubble up.
Spinning tales of yesteryears,
These moments melt away the fears.

Every mishap, a chance to cheer,
With tickle fights that bring us near.
Our hearts entwined, though far apart,
In every jest, you steal my heart.

We'll ride this rocket through the skies,
With silly dreams no one denies.
In every joke and playful tease,
We find our happiness with ease!

Tied by Fate

Two hearts met on a crowded street,
With tangled shoes, they tripped and beat.
A silly dance, a laughter spree,
Fate twisted them, oh how funny!

In coffee shops, they spilled their drinks,
Swapping stories, exchanging winks.
Love's clumsy game, they're in the race,
With every stumble, they find their place.

The Heart's Embroidery

A stitch in time, a heart-shaped patch,
Sewing love with a crazy catch.
A frayed old quilt of different hues,
Threads of laughter where love brews.

Each knot a tale, a silly pun,
Woven together, they're never done.
They tangle up in a fabric flat,
Caught in threads, like two curious cats.

Love's Intricate Patterns

In the dance of socks that never match,
Love's patterns form, each step a catch.
With polka dots and stripes galore,
A fashion show that begs for more!

They paint a canvas with splashed delight,
Each brushstroke wrong feels perfectly right.
In mismatched prints, their hearts collide,
A whirlwind laughter, no need to hide.

Unbroken Links

Two peas in a pod, rolling downhill,
Laughing so hard, they've lost their chill.
Each link they make is forged in fun,
With every giggle, they're always spun.

Unbroken chains of inside jokes,
Tangled in laughter, like playful folks.
They gather friends with their quirky charms,
Creating memories, spread wide their arms.

Cords of Companionship

Two socks in the dryer, they dance and they spin,
A friendship that started with a tumble within.
Like bread and like butter, they spread out their cheer,
Who knew laundry could bring us so near?

In the world of lost items, we searched with a grin,
A pair of old shoes, and we laughed 'til we'd win.
We share all our secrets like kids on a swing,
With every silly moment, our hearts start to sing.

Bridging the Distance

A phone call from miles, your voice like a breeze,
We joke through the static and share our unease.
The Wi-Fi is shaky, but laughter's a must,
Who needs perfect signals when there's friendship and trust?

A postcard you sent, my fridge is the muse,
With doodles and puns, how could I refuse?
From coffee spills to travel mishaps in tow,
We bridge all the gaps with the stories we know.

The Art of Together

In the kitchen we gather, a floury mess,
Baking would fail, but we still feel blessed.
Eggs on the ceiling, the laughter just flies,
Somehow burnt biscuits become our surprise.

We try every dance, a spectacle grand,
Two left feet fumble, yet we understand.
Mirror ball spins as we trip, hop, and sway,
It's silly, but hey, it brightens the day!

Weaving Memories

With crayons and paper, we craft dreams so bright,
A masterpiece showing our wildest delight.
Each scribble a memory, each color a song,
Who knew art could be so ridiculously wrong?

With games that we play, like charades in the night,
Miming our stories, we giggle with fright.
A mix of lost words, and wild gestures delight,
Together we shine, in this comical fight.

Heartbeats Entwined

In a dance of skips and hops,
Our hearts play games, never stops.
With silly faces, we collide,
Like mismatched socks taking pride.

Tickles echo in the air,
Jumping jacks with hearts laid bare.
A sneeze brings laughter to our lunch,
Who knew love could pack a punch?

We sing off-key, but who cares?
Our duo's charm, beyond compare.
With laughter fizzing like champagne,
In quirks, we find our sweet refrain.

In playful jests, we intertwine,
Beneath the moon, it feels divine.
Like clumsy puppies on a spree,
Together, love's a comedy!

The Bridge of Unspoken Words

Between our brows, a language flows,
With winks and grins, the rhythm grows.
Each eyebrow raise, a secret told,
In silent laughter, we unfold.

Your quirks, they light the dullest day,
Unraveled webs of what we say.
A laugh so loud, it turns the tide,
With every nod, my heart's your guide.

Puns fly high, like kites in spring,
The silly joy that you bring.
Through tangled thoughts, we share a glance,
In clumsy chats, we find our dance.

Our bridge extends, no words required,
In giggles shared, our love's inspired.
With each eye-roll, we build anew,
Our silent talks, a love so true.

Sentiments Spiraled

In spirals made of silly glee,
Your heart's a meme that laughs with me.
With each twist, the giggles climb,
Unraveling joy, a silly rhyme.

Like spaghetti flung with flair,
Our love is messy, yet we care.
You trip, I laugh, it's quite the show,
Our clumsy love steals every glow.

In circles round, we chase our tails,
With jolly tales and giggling gales.
Silly hats and colors bright,
In our own world, we take flight.

With every twist, a giggle born,
Life's a circus, the laugh keeps warm.
Through wild rides and ups and downs,
Our love's the silliest of crowns.

Dreamscapes of Affection

In a dream, we float on clouds,
Wrapped in blankets, giggling loud.
With goofy grins, we drift and sway,
In our sweet dreams, we laugh and play.

Bouncing on stars, we skip the night,
In candy worlds, everything's right.
You steal my popcorn, I just smirk,
In these dreamscapes, we go berserk.

With cotton candy in our grasp,
We dance in skies, no time to gasp.
Every hiccup brings laughter near,
In these soft dreams, there's naught to fear.

With sleepy sighs and dreams entwined,
We chase the giggles, always kind.
In our mosaic of moonlit sights,
Love's an adventure filled with bites.

The Art of Attachment

In a world where socks lose their pairs,
Love's a game, full of playful snares.
With coffee spills and cheeky grins,
We dance through life on our silly whims.

Each text you send, a giggling tease,
You stick like glue, on my funny knees.
Like pasta twisted on a fork,
We laugh at love, our own quirky cork.

Not all superheroes wear a cape,
Some just wear slippers, and that's their shape.
With inside jokes and a winked eye,
We're the laughter on the roller-coaster sky.

So here's to us, the oddball crew,
Who trip on love, but never rue.
With every bump, we bounce and roll,
Mastering the art of fun-filled soul.

Hidden Harmonies

In a cluttered room with mismatched socks,
You find the humor in each paradox.
With a cereal box as your makeshift crown,
You wear your laughter like a whimsical gown.

Discordant tunes in our cozy nest,
Yet somehow we make the silliest fest.
With spatulas dancing, and fruits in the air,
We hum our secrets without a care.

In the quiet chaos, love's rhythm hums,
It's spontaneous giggles and wobbly drums.
When you trip on my toe, we both burst out,
In hidden harmonies, love's what it's about.

So let's sing loud, with off-key delight,
As we waltz through the odd, through day and night.
In this crazy dance, with stumbles so sweet,
We've found our tune, love's silly heartbeat.

Unseen Threads

Invisible strings tie up our laughs,
In the oddest ways, like two silly halves.
You drop my sandwich, I spill your drink,
Together we wobble, we never sink.

Like cats in a box, we twist and turn,
With playful jabs, our hearts brightly burn.
A rubber band love that stretches and spins,
In mismatched shoes, we wear goofy grins.

Your jokes are the glue, that binds our play,
In the grand circus of our everyday.
With humor our armor, we face each mess,
Tangled together, we feel truly blessed.

So here's to the laughter, the clumsy ballet,
In unseen threads, we find our way.
A tapestry woven of joyous sighs,
In this quirky quilt, our love never dies.

Captured in Moments

In a snapshot of chaos, we flash a smile,
Captured in moments, each funny style.
With your spaghetti hair and my pie in the face,
We freeze the laughter in our silly space.

From silly selfies to pratfall scenes,
Our life's a comedy, bursting at the seams.
You pull a prank, I jump with glee,
In this gallery of giggles, it's just you and me.

With every mishap, a new tale unfolds,
A scrapbook of stories, more precious than gold.
Your memes invade my phone every day,
Each notification, a chuckle ballet.

So let's snap away, in this endless spree,
Captured in moments, where we're wild and free.
In every frame, let's keep it bright,
A soft photo finish in our love's delight.

Threads of Memory

In a closet, old shirts lay,
Each a tale, come what may.
Mom's favorite '80s design,
I swear it still smells like wine.

My buddy thought he could sew,
Into the fashion world he'd go.
But mismatched buttons all around,
Make a catwalk a silly sound.

Grandpa's socks in every shade,
Bright as the jokes that he's made.
He wears them with such great pride,
While grandma just rolls her eyes wide.

Memory threads, so twisted and frayed,
Tugging us back to the games we played.
Spools of laughter, sorrow, and fun,
Sewing our stories, each stitch a pun.

Harmonious Unions

Two left shoes, a comical pair,
On a dance floor without a care.
One goes left and one goes right,
Tap dance twirls turn into flight.

Frogs and turtles form a band,
With croaks and hops that sound so grand.
Stringy tails and slicky shells,
Their melody rings like dinner bells.

A cat and a mouse, friends through and through,
Playing tag with a comical view.
Around the sofa, they scamper and chase,
Inventing new games in the silliest place.

Bees buzz a tune, flowers sway along,
In a garden of laughter, we all belong.
With a wink and a nudge, we dance through time,
Creating life's rhythms, sweet and sublime.

The Interlace of Longing

A spaghetti strand, long and thin,
Noodles tangled, where to begin?
Sauce spills over, a puddle, oh dear,
An Italian dinner turns into cheer.

Paperclips stuck in a wild twist,
Chasing dreams, but something's amiss.
Each a curve, a different way,
But all together, they still play.

Kites in the sky, a windy ballet,
Tethered and pulling, they sway away.
Yet down below, a dog is barking,
Chasing cotton candy, is he embarking?

From far away, I hear my phone,
My pizza's arrived, now I'm never alone.
Stringing together this tasty delight,
With each cheesy bite, life feels just right.

Enchanted Touch

A tickle fight on a rainy day,
Clouds giggle, and the puddles play.
We jump and splash, laughter galore,
Magical moments we can't ignore.

Fairy lights in the garden's glow,
We dance like fireflies, in a row.
With a wink from the moon, mischievous and bright,
All our worries take flight into the night.

A hug from a teddy, so fluffy and round,
He whispers secrets, his heartbeats abound.
When things feel heavy, he's always on call,
With a squeeze and a smirk, he conquers it all.

In a world full of quirks, where mishaps unite,
It's a tapestry woven, a colorful sight.
Laughter we borrow, love we bestow,
In this enchanted dance, together we flow.

Relations Woven in Time

In a dance of quirks, we play,
Our bloopers brighten every day.
Laughing at moments we might regret,
A patchwork of joy, we won't forget.

With socks that clash and shoes askew,
Our style's a riot, but love shines through.
Like mismatched puzzle pieces we fit,
Creating a picture, we freely admit.

Time's a comedian, pulling our strings,
With every joke, a new smile springs.
We roll our eyes, then share a laugh,
Life's ticklish moments, our silly path.

So here's to the bonds that make us bold,
In laughter and mishaps, our stories unfold.
With each silly twist, our hearts will climb,
Forever stitched in this laughable rhyme.

The Heart's Compass

With a wink and a nod, we roam,
Finding our way back to home.
A funny map of trust and cheer,
Navigating nonsense, we hold dear.

You stole my fries, I took your drink,
In every mischief, we pause and think.
Our hearts are magnets, drawing near,
In a world of chuckles, it's all quite clear.

Like two lost socks in a dryer's spin,
Unraveling whirlwinds where giggles begin.
In misadventures, we learn and grow,
Together, we bask in life's silly glow.

So let's chart our course through laughter's tide,
With every quirk, let love be our guide.
In this merry dance, we gleefully play,
With hearts aligned, come what may.

When Words Entwine

In rambling chats, our thoughts collide,
Crafting tales where punchlines hide.
Your silly phrases, a comic gold,
A friendship that never gets old.

We argue over pizza toppings, a riot,
Silent exchanges felt in the quiet.
Your quirky puns pull me tight,
In our dialogue, pure delight.

In whispers that tickle and teasing gripes,
Through playful banter, the heartpipes.
Creating a melody, we freely sing,
In this laughter, joy takes wing.

So here's to the words that weave our bond,
In this lighthearted jest, we respond.
Each chuckle a thread, pulling us near,
With language sweet as a cuddle, my dear.

Symphony of Silences

In silence, we share a knowing glance,
An echo of laughter, our secret dance.
With faces aglow, oh what a scene,
Each tickle of humor, so light and keen.

Your raised eyebrow speaks a thousand lines,
In the stillness, our humor shines.
Like quiet giggles hiding in a nook,
The spaces between are where the joy took.

With moments that shimmer, yet fall so flat,
Each quiet chuckle, a stylish spat.
Our silent symphony, a riotous tune,
Playing together, afternoon into moon.

So here's to the quiet, unmatched delight,
In the echoes and pauses, the hearts take flight.
A melody crafted, where laughter resides,
In the symphony of silences, love abides.

www.ingramcontent.com/pod-product-compliance
Lightning Source LLC
Chambersburg PA
CBHW051733290426
43661CB00123B/255